HARMING
OTHERS

# HARMING OTHERS

POEMS BY
Casey Finch

The University of Georgia Press

Athens and London

Published by the University of Georgia Press
Athens, Georgia 30602
Designed by Betty McDaniel
Set in Meridien
The paper in this book meets the guidelines for
permanence and durability of the Committee on
Production Guidelines for Book Longevity of the
Council on Library Resources.

Printed in the United States of America
96   95   94   93   92      C      5   4   3   2   1
96   95   94   93   92      P      5   4   3   2   1

Library of Congress Cataloging in Publication Data

Finch, Casey.
   Harming others : poems / by Casey Finch.
      p. cm.
   ISBN 0-8203-1373-4 (alk. paper).—ISBN 0-8203-1374-2
(pbk. : alk. paper)
   I. Title.                    11/11/92
PS3556.I454H3   1992
811'.54—dc20          91–14149
                         CIP


British Library Cataloging in Publication Data available

## ACKNOWLEDGMENTS

The author and publisher gratefully acknowledge the following publications in which these poems, sometimes in earlier versions, first appeared:

*Berkeley Poetry Review:* "Dear Kenneth," "The Forbidden Poems"
*Hawai'i Review:* "Treatise," "The *Iliad*," "Year One"
*Iowa Review:* "England," "Rome"
*Mississippi Review:* "Thomas Edison"
*Ohio Review:* "Against Poetics," "Midnight"
*Pegasus:* "Greece"
*Ploughshares:* "Egypt"
*River Styx:* "The Problem of Fun"

My sincere appreciation goes out to Nancy Kricorian and James Schamus; the effort they dedicated to promoting this collection left them with less time to pursue their own (superior) writing.

The publication of this book is supported by a grant from the National Endowment for the Arts, a federal agency.

# CONTENTS

## 2. New

Part One

# THE
# EMPIRE
# POEMS

# 1)
# ROME

He was civilized and grievous. On the thin,
uncelebrated day he died, the sparrows flew out
like an opened fist, dragging the invisible sky
behind them. The sparrows flew out in idiotic
formation, as in cartoons, and together sang
an old and awkward song; though out of it came
nothing. For in the provinces the chained and
frozen rivers did nothing when the news of it
arrived. The aqueducts stood, as always, immovable
in the televised wind. No fire dismantled the
olive groves. No roads began to break apart

or disappear. He was civilized and grievous.
He used to intercept the orders the air gave
to the trees, to string the stars themselves
into a corrupt astrology that placed at the
center of the tiniest, most distant things
his sword and shining brow. But on the
unrecorded day he died, nothing was stolen or
noticed. No one wrote a single elegy or tugged
madly at his hair. No satellites swerved
from their marvelous orbits across the Roman sky.

He was gifted and good to look at. He was
civilized and grievous and lean. He used to
stand at the control board of battles, to stare,
magnificent and horny, at the borders of
countries whose names he could not pronounce,
and there decide what of the earth he would push
aside and what he would build into another

lousy road. But on the day he died, the poems
and the lies he commissioned returned to nothing,
hollow now and useless. Nothing was harmed or
misplaced. No quarrels were interrupted. And
in the afternoon no provinces gathered to form a
geography of mourning. It was impossible to
dislike or ignore him, for he drank too much and
wept at his own happiness. It was impossible
to forget the beautiful, inconsistent language
he pushed down the throats of his enemies.
He was civilized and cheerful. He was

beautiful and abrasive and worthy. But when
he died, when the good times became too good
to untangle, nothing bore his body on a shield
or broadcast the news of it to the provinces.
Nothing refilled the vending machines he set up
at the crossroads. And, in the end, nothing
came down on a wind from the north and
dropped leaves into his wide, ridiculous grave.

## 2)

# GREECE

After Odysseus Elytis' "Song for the Lost
2nd Lieutenant of the Albanian Campaign"

She was ugly. On the last day of her death
the fields of Athens stood upright to hide
the unhappy wheat on the loins of the loose earth.
The fields of Athens stood up and kissed her
once on the foot, once on the shoulder blades,
and once for the strange fun of it all.
Soldiers came home with their lovely traps
and lowered her down into a grave.
And the nights walked forward to see
the bottom of the sky where the clouds
moved off. The evening brooks
stopped following their old, dried trails.
She was ugly. She used to clean the huge coat
of the planets and stroke the moon on the frame
of a tree until dusk could not find her
or pour the darkness into her eyes. Dusk
who with closed fists would throw
its vultures across her weak sky.

What a landscape of shame her covered face
on which fields and slavery closed!
She was ugly with her bright shields,
with her boots and rivers a dull gray,
with her civilians above and below.

## 3)
## EGYPT


She was abrupt and glad, like an ostrich.
On the day of her death, the Nile got up
and tore at its hair in astonishment and
grief. The Nile got up and walked abroad and
wept and argued and spread upon the desert
first a shroud of water and then a shroud

of endless clay. She was unaccountable
and glad. She used to build power lines
across the Sahara, to broadcast through the
evening sky the stories of her courage
and acquisitions. Too many guns were
fashioned, too many ghetto blasters and
shitty houses. Too many jokes and sacrifices
were performed, acts at once beneath her
and endless, like killing a dog, a thing
ignoble, a thing at last not very hard to do.

But now she's gone. Now the racetracks
and amusement parks are closed, and the
winds that sang her name, pathetically
and well, cut through the discarded record
stores and concession stands until there is
nothing left but a handful of anecdotes
and lies. Now the stars each night stare
through the perfect window of the sea
into the earth's obscene interior,
and there number the men and the farm
equipment she destroyed when she was glad
and unstoppable. Now there is nothing left

but departments of music and literature.
And in the evening, the shadows cast by
the blank, unfumigated buildings push
themselves sadly and ridiculously beyond
the horizons, finally sick of the worn-out
jokes and the Egyptian game shows. She was

ample and magnificent and funny. But on the
interpreted day she died, the sun, which she
had turned into a god, hid its head beneath
the stupid hills; the earth, confused as it
was, finally decided that it disliked her
and wanted its big toys back; and the green,
upturned torso of the sea prayed again
for the scalding rain to drop and make it clean.

## 4)
## ENGLAND

He was alert and sad, like a sparrow.
On the day of his death, the rain
was merciless and tore, with its thousand
hooks, at the forests and the plowlands.
The rain was merciless and cold, as
in elegies, and broken umbrellas lay
like bats along the roads, with wind-
inverted ribs, abandoned, twisting and
flexing in the invisible air. On the
day of his death, for a tiny moment,
all the visionaries stopped shuffling
their marked, mysterious decks of
cards and gave back, to their customers,
the coins they had stolen. And in
the afternoon, the poets, happy to
seize on the fresh material, carried
the news of it to the drunken kings
of Northumbria:
                    how, when he fought,
the sparks that rose from the
blade of his battle-axe covered
the canopy of stars, the sparks that
rose were counted, one by one, and
took their fixed, significant places in
the stories of his outrage and courage;
how, robbed at last of his friends
and retainers, he stared out, dumbly, from
the solitude of the mead hall;
how, in the end, an animal broke his
spine in two, like a cardboard shirt-

liner from the cleaners; how the companions-
in-arms gathered together and bore his
body on a shield over the blackened hills;
and how, at dusk, the sun, a kind of
old and rusted pinball, fell gracelessly
out of the air, down a ramp, and back
into the terrible belly of the earth. Dusk
which smelled like his last meal of
lamb raised by the labor of peasants
whose farms he sacked when he was bored
and ambitious.
    He was alert and sad.
He used to stretch the evening sky across
the lands he brought his battles to,
to make of blood an ocean and throw the
bodies of his enemies there, until the waves
began to groan and plead that he
release them, until the waves were choked
with the deaths of men he might have
liked, he might have fed and entertained
at great expense.
    He was strong and loved
to brag and pity himself. He was alert
and sad, like a sparrow. Once all the
crouched halls of the countryside shook
with the episodes of his cruelty. Once
the moon itself grew hot and breathless
when his sword and shining loins
sparkled in the light with which it
followed him around, like a dog.
      But now
he's gone. Now the mead halls are emptied
of their criminals and their feasts.
Only a handful of men continue the lies
he initiated. And of the sons they

send forth onto the bombed-out battle-
fields, into the torched buildings,
fewer and fewer remember the noisy,
unreluctant man whose hands and breath
stank of mead, who, delicate and insane,
pushed countries about with his feet, whose
laughter was so frightening and rare.

Part Two

# THE
# DAMAGED
# POEMS

# AGAINST POETICS

October sits on an artificial rock in
Central Park, leering
at the couples moving by. All around,
the trees are exchanging compliments,
nodding to one another in the unnoticeable
breeze, casting out ropes from their
uppermost boughs, like great ships
in harbors heaving to. Inertia

is always like this: climbing over a
hill in Central Park; its hands in
its pockets; blinking dumbly at the
raised prices of the pretzel vendors;
and staring out, beyond the statues
and the reservoir, into the calendrical
expanse of rain, as if at the impossibility
of seeing things distinctly. Power

and architecture walk hand in hand along
a promenade, smiling drunkenly at
one another, their pockets full of money.
Meanwhile the wind pulls itself through
the branches like a chain. Meanwhile
the sky holds up its paper fists and
threatens to lecture and to sing to us.
You can hear, in the distance, the stroke
and counterstroke of damage
autumn does to softball fields and
reputations, and overhead, faintly
crackling, the undecipherable law
the stars hold out along with hands

of ancient light. But who would not
applaud this grandiose kind
of procrastination? For though nothing
happens, the parade of chimeras nevertheless
moves unhaltingly by. There are trees
around us to confuse us, texts, ghetto
blasters, things to eat, different kinds
of love. Yet October is always
like this. Pieces of trash float by,
tied together by an invisible thread.
You whisper something ignominious in
quotation marks. Traffic continues
down the broken ramp of politics
around you. And overhead,
unfailingly, the days and nights are hung
like lanterns on an endless string.

# MARRIAGE

An Epithalamion for Melissa Spielman
and Richard Lawrence

September is dismantling the empty summer sky,
erecting in the morning a vast scaffolding
around it, hanging mirrors from its walls all
afternoon, and in the evening sending epithalamions
through the dark, unholy air: the first signs of
things gone wrong. But meanwhile the sentimental
refuses to be either intimidated or inspired
by any of this, continuing, for instance, to
devour the paperbacks, happily unaware of their
conclusions. And in the end, if it feels like it,
it keeps on getting good and married, as if
marriage were not at once the end and the
beginning of something grandiose and therefore

beyond us. But what if marriage turns out to
be a kind of infinite train we agree to take
across an infinite countryside, the inconsequential
roads and farmhouses receding forever from memory,
receding forever into the huge architecture of
what we did not choose and therefore cannot have?
What if marriage is in fact a form of improvisational
art, at once ferocious and impermanent and therefore
sublime; or only something axiomatic and slightly
dull, like a law of science about to be replaced,
about to snap under the weight of being fragile and
emblematic? There is enough in the sheer order
of things to keep marriages from tampering with
what is sad and necessary. Did you really think
it could mean hiking miles through the unrolling

Northumbrian countryside, never feeling thirsty,
and noticing every other year the shadow of a
new child striding beside you, her hand placed
delicately in yours?
                              Did you really think
that happiness could be chosen, as though it
were a favorite color? Meanwhile the Septembers,
as they roll dumbly by, will continue ripping
the artichokes from the fields with their
bloody fingers, firing up their chainsaws, and
clambering like vandals to the treetops. And
meanwhile, those of us who remain unmarried will
muddle on, still bouncing checks, still knocking
over liquor stores in the beautiful, uneven light
of American afternoons. And all of it done
as though you two had not fallen ludicrously
in love, had not made a habit of exchanging oaths
at one another's thighs, as though you had not tied
your lives into a kind of symbol of what is good
and unforgettable and ceremonious and glad.

# MIDNIGHT

Ainsi, pour le lecteur, tout est à
faire et tout est déjà fait.

— SARTRE

This is called a poem. It wants you
to recognize it first by its presence
in language; then by the frame
the title gives it; then by its
irregular right margin; then by the
way it refers to its own procedures;
and last by its first sentence,
which it quotes, "This is called a

poem." By now it imagines you
thinking, "Language can't account for
its own procedures—so why bother?"
or, "I'm almost old and almost
happy." Either way the poem is

pleased; it pictures you sitting at
a table in the kitchen, sipping a
beer, and being kind to someone you
almost love. The steam from your
cooking has clouded the windows. There's
a lamp, a vase of bluebells, and a
chewed-up *Paradise Lost* at your elbow.
It pictures you, naked at midnight,
scooping catfood into a glass bowl
on the floor and, later on, sleeping
happily on a rooftop, sleeping happily

in the dry, brightly lit night air.
You are this poem's procedures. You
sleep, for a while, in the web the stars
weave out of old, domestic light.

# YEAR ONE

For Ann Law on Her Birthday

Lately I have given up on birthdays, and have
taken, instead, to wandering up and down the sad,
unchanging avenues of growing up, to stopping in
at the department stores, because of the poised,
unlucky promises their windows hold out like
brightly colored birthday presents. I suppose
I've grown afraid of the doomed, rickety
architecture that birthdays build; afraid the
soaring scaffolding would collapse one year under
the wear and tear of making empty promises,
under the sheer weight of the ordinary and the

boring. But I imagine you are somehow more fearless
and relaxed. I imagine you calling up a birthday
on the telephone and giving it advice. I imagine
you shaping it in your image, the way you would
make a dance or a point in a conversation you
no longer believed in, even though it is late
at night, and the March wind as it moves through
your window carries with it the iciness and broken
branches of the unspeakable, even though each
birthday confronts you with the shitty, unmodulated
rhythm of self-recognition. You are far better at
birthdays than most of us. You hail them like
taxis in a rush-hour rain. And they pull up at
the curb, obediently, one by one, forever eager to
take you where you wish, because they, too, are
aging, because they, too, are poised and strong.

# THOMAS EDISON

It is only on a cross that a man dies
with his arms outstretched.

— ORIGEN

He grew up ugly, color-blind, masturbating, touching
Everything: pinwheels, faucets, pumps, the eye
Sockets of nickelodeons, the invisible rivers of

Air that pushed sunlight through the high, crossed
Girders of the railway stations of Ohio.
They trounced him with insults, they notified

His mother. But o undaunted, he rose through his
Flowcharts, equations, print messages like a fiend!
He dismantled a piano, a grandfather clock,

A combine harvester. He tore off his shirts and bit
His lips. He ate paste and spat in a bag.
They canceled his checks and made obscene

Gestures. But o unfailing, he turned over his
Electric coils like tiny diamonds in a cave!
He built a page turner, a mercury scale, he fashioned

A pocket blowtorch. They threw him from a train
And diluted his soup. Anything for a gag, a hound, a
Pilfer. Anything for a pin, a crease, a pockmark

In his glory. But o unstopping, he constructed
A two-holed camera, a swivel bolt, a scope chart!
He gripped at the air and picked at his shoes.

He designed the signal transfer, the can, the can
Opener. He devoured newspapers, tore leaves
Down their spine, and glued together marbles,

Pieces of skin, insects' legs, the tails of cats.
O unappreciated! A toothpick, a magazine, a night bat,
The smallest unkind glance would set him thinking.

They raised his rent, they canned him, they recoiled.
But o despite them, the future in its fat, important
Chair eyed him up and down and lit another cigar.

# DEAR KENNETH

I got your letter just this afternoon.
It wasn't nice of you to raise the rent
To ten percent above what we agreed;
And though you are "within your rights," as you're
So fond of saying, still, somehow, it seems
A trust of sorts is violated by
This new request. Or should I say it seems
To me? At any rate I wanted to
Respond.
          I want to say I'm happy that
You like me "as a tenant," hope, in fact,
That I'll "continue on." I even think
I understand you when you write, "I feel
It's only natural resisting change,
But change we must!" *Alas,* my friend, is what
They used to say in situations that
Are sad but unavoidable. Increase
Of rent, I guess, is one of these. But your
Analogy of continents for change,
With which you seemed so pleased, still baffles me:
"If continents," your letter added, "drift
Apart, forever changing neighborhoods,
And seem contented, why should we complain
About a couple dollars here or there
Or contemplate a move?" But isn't that,
I have to ask, what continents would do
If someone raised *their* rent: pack up and start
An inching exodus away from what
They could no longer tolerate?

And if
You like analogy then take one I
Prefer: the habits of deciduous trees
That open new, expensive blossoms each
Unfailing spring and throw them off each fall
*But only grudgingly!* How would they
Respond if someone raised by ten percent
The cost of being trees? You really think
They'd take it stoically and not complain?

But, Kenneth, if you look at continents
And trees a little longer you'll admit
That like most things they don't hold up, not as
Analogies at least. For everything,
It seems, both likes to stay intact and yet
Exhibits change, and could be called upon
To prove what point you wished.
                              And so, in this,
I only want to let you know that as
Of now I've given "thirty days" and both
Resist and somehow welcome such a change.

# HARMING OTHERS

Puppets are a way we have of talking
to one another, as we get older.
— JIM HENSON

Time in December gets confused, like
a man, blind drunk and old, trying to sleep
in a vast expanse of snow. Each night
the bus routes are rearranged, cruelly
and mysteriously. And each morning the sun
begins again the outrageous effort merely
to rise, merely to hang suspended a
handful of hours in the blank, unthoughtful
air. And that's one of the reasons
the month makes us feel at once satisfied and
disappointed, why it makes us forgetful,
and in the end takes back the little promises
that had taken us in all year. How

expansive and silly everything in December
is! Last night, for instance, I thought
of calling you and, a few TV shows later, of
letting it be: the Christmas programming had
made me stupid and weepy; and anyway at midnight
*Miracle on 34th Street* was rolling by!

Time in December gets suspended like the
regular programming. Someone has cast great
ropes around it and pulled it, with the
last of the leaves, just beyond the football
fields, someone trying to be popular
and witty, like the boys in my high school

who one night over Christmas vacation hung
the giant pine tree before the gym with
a hundred shopping carts, the enterprise,
like art, at once massive and unhelpful.

# SPAIN

For Peter Bowen on His Departure

I like to think of the sad, surprising postcards
you will doubtless fail to send to me from Spain,
neglecting, as usual, to put strings of X's and
O's on the bottom of what you do not write and
do not send. They miss me, I imagine, and find
a thousand ways to be flattering and buoyant, like
all the words that, before I had a phone machine,
friends might have said to me when they called and

I was out. There is little difference between
travelling and writing home about travelling.
No matter; I like to think of you anyway, dazed
by the sunlight, your eyes the color of the
afternoon, your fingers leafing nervously through
a pocket dictionary, searching for a word you cannot
find, or sleeping somewhere past dawn in an empty
room, a bag of unsent postcards beside the bed:
reproductions of El Grecos and photos of
Gibraltar—clichés in other words—one or two
already stamped, sounding forlorn and broke, another
describing your suntan, and still another a dream you
had, in which you found yourself hiding in the
shops of a medieval city whose cathedral housed
Franco's troops one winter, and whose streets
were so tangled and small they could not even
accommodate a single shadow. There is nothing

that is not the country you are travelling across,
half-lost, half-hitchhiking in the dust and the
Andalusian sunlight, while the German families
roar by at illegal speeds, their teenagers
yelling mockingly from the windows, as though
admonishing you for failing to consider those
friends at home who love so much to think of you
this way, for failing, as usual, simply to
write. Why? No doubt because the coffee and
the morning light have made you pleased for a
while and forgetful; because the pictures on
the only postcards you've purchased so far are
"homosexual," which is precisely what you are
thinking I am *not;* and because, having
"better" things to do, you are anxiously planning
the day's travels, studying the *cañadas* on a
map whose dangers you are unable to translate.

# THE *ILIAD*

Everything is difficult to see in New York,
precisely because it is so visible. You can
be standing before one of the largest and
ugliest buildings in the world and fail to
notice. For meanwhile the taxis continue to
weave their infinite web of usefulness
around you; mailmen drag the afternoon along
on endless ropes; and in the evening, the
locked-up stores throw trapezoids of light
along the streets. Though everything unfolds
in its bright uniqueness, meanwhile,
as always, one fails to notice. But this

is how it is on earth: half the time you
dream about dreaming; the other half, as
Richard Rorty says, "you dream about
claiming to be awake." Even in the *Iliad,*

for instance, no one notices the gods
anymore, because noticing is unhelpful and
too sagacious. The women walk along the
streets of Troy, under the orange glow of
the streetlights, past the boarded-up
department stores, staring vacantly at their
sandals. Beyond the walls, along the stretched-
out battlefield, the men push to and fro
all night; and the movement is gloomy and sexual
and wears a kind of cape. And unrecognizably,
like the first, distant strokes of
lightning above a wheatfield near
Omaha, once in a while their tiny voices

are raised: the exchange of family names,
insults, traces of identity. Each sound
sparkles in the vast Nebraska air. No one
remembers the words of Agamemnon before
the ships. No one thinks of anything, but
gathering in the frightened cows and the last
of the sheets stretching back the laundry
line like a great bowstring about to snap.
Meanwhile, with the clouds, the vastness
and inexhaustibility of the ordinary gather
on the horizon. And when the rain begins
delicately to sparkle on the shop windows along
Madison Avenue, Homer himself shoves an old
woman aside and, just as her brightly colored
packages burst open on the curb, hails
one of the last available taxis, the news
of it tucked under his thin and ancient arm.

# TREATISE

For Susan Adams on Her Birthday

There are apple trees in New York City.
I have seen them, swaying their heads
like paper in the recent air, trying
to look graceful by showing their crowns
in the imperfect light. Clouds gather
above them to applaud and flirt with one
another. Clouds gather above them on
trapeze wires, doing handstands in the
sunlight, backflips, somersaults,
reaching down for the blossoms which they
take in their hands and juggle, madly,
and then grow tired of, and throw down
to the floor of the apple forests.

I wish all this could somehow rearrange
itself for your birthday. I wish the city
itself could get up off its broken back
and be prodigal and entertaining. But
after all New York has its vast self-
appointment to keep; and everything
continues as if it were not your birthday,
as if it had other business to attend,
the wear and tear of its own life to
consider.
   The grammar of time is a
terrible thing. The people it pulls
under its canopy, like you and me,
were only trying to help, to account
for the thousand words we bring like

gifts to one another. It is sad,
this colorful, blindfolded parade of birthdays,
this business of gathering years in your
arms and then throwing them away, one by
one, as if they were bad poems. But
you are stronger than all of this. My
guess is that you stack like newspapers
the crowded, diminishing, unserious days,
their fingers blackened with ink, only
to recycle them, only to write, years later,
long unsentimental letters to their
editors, because they, too, have birthdays,
because they, too, are transient.
                                    I hope
you see the apple trees before the season
moves off and leaves them hanging like curtains
in the blank and ruined air. They are
more informative than beautiful. They
sway all night like fences in the wind,
signs at last of how hard it is
to be graceful, to watch the clouds reach
down into the apple boughs and then
move off with their arms full of blossoms.

# GAWAIN AND THE LADY

Well, she took a bad night personally and grace-
lessly wept; and as she twisted in the bedsheets,
she tired him with the old clichés of medieval
poetry: "When God, Who starved, finally gets a

good soup, He'll not borrow any coins from you,
unhappy sir!" Not that one so good as Gawain
the Sloppy is unhoused so easily! For nothing
himself—the very point of politeness—he excludes
his body even to holiness. So gamesome a gentleman
couldn't simply have bolted without a hated smack
on the lips or two, bum that he is. But by a
tactless indiscretion, her thoughts wandered from
this and that, and afterwards she sighed and forgot
the idiot again, exclaiming insanely (as behooves
such a salty hag): "I'll never kiss any weapon
of yours. And even less (I hope this irks you),
though you ask and ask and ask!" So she pried
from her skin the blasted fiend and threw him
from her legs and, grossly straightening up,
miserably, he licked her one last time and, thus doing,
nonverbally recommended them both to lower hell!

Well, with lots of filly-fallying over and under
the sheets, he forwarded and arrived; and she
fell back into a swoon and slowly made herself,
after many pauses, available. And, well, they
prayed to their God and licked one another's
fingers and in the end slinked back to another

religious festival. And when Gawain finally came
from that banquet that could no longer put up
with his jokes, he was utterly forlorn for the
nightlong, before the sun crawled out from under
the dirt and stared at him as he rode endlessly
away in a countryside flattened and damp and strewn
with abandoned gas stations. And she, the wilted
bag, packed her things and went miserably home.

# TRICKS

(1)
She jerked off in a full-length mirror; it
was a form of mourning and a form of joy.

(2)
Where had it begun, this erection
that now held him in its clamp?

(3)
Licking Ariadne's cunt, she realized how hungry she
was: always the confusion of food & sex & solitude.

(4)
He was only interested in paying
for sex, and not in sex.

(5)
She fucked him in German, in French, in
Italian, but no tongue was wet enough.

(6)
It was a gesture of solitude,
like drinking milk from a condom.

(7)
He always fucked fully dressed; the
unbrutal bored him, along with pleasure.

(8)
She got off on phone sex; otherwise it was
impossible to smile and come simultaneously.

(9)
His cunt was the color of pink
grapefruit; hers of a midsummer plum.

(10)
She fucked him in the ass while he slept;
it was the only way to notice time passing.

(11)
His cock was a hammer in my backside,
his name a shadow on my tongue.

# THE PROBLEM OF FUN

> One of these days I'm going to build an
> amusement park—and it's going to be clean!
> — WALT DISNEY, 1920

It's confusing to be so happy. One minute
you're fast-forwarding through the dialogue
in a porn movie, and the next you're counting
your winnings at the racetrack, dollar bills
floating down around you. In the dawn light

you wander up and down the streets, your
pockets full of credit cards, buying clothes
and having fun, feeling horny as always,
enough to make you angry. The sun hangs in
its usual seizures above you. The water levels
in the reservoirs climb and drop, as though
breathing very very slowly. The beautiful,
surprised manikins continue to stare helplessly
out from the store windows along Madison
Avenue, as if at the sheer damage done
by the recklessness called "shopping" or "joy."

And the hot afternoons rumble by like airplanes
over Jones Beach, trailing bright banners
behind them: ads, movie listings, baseball
scores, 900 numbers for phone sex services.
You stare across from one luminous space
of happiness to another, your fingers sore
from signing bad checks, your heart still clogged
with astonishing hope. Sometimes I wonder if fun
will eventually hurt itself, like a boy standing

in a roller coaster, waving his arms and screaming
to catch the attention of his mother waiting below.

Can fun be divided like summer pie and dispersed
equally amongst a large picnic party, even
though all the guests are not equally nice?
Probably. And that's the trouble. That's
the reason for the poem. Can fun be collected
systematically like baseball cards or shells from
the beach? Probably not. That's why we
trivialize it, preferring to imagine ourselves
outside its call, or beyond its stupid grip.

# EPITHALAMION

For Megan Ratner and Thad Meyerriecks

A meet and happy conversation is the chiefest
and noblest end of marriage.

— MILTON

These nights are absolutely "quiet," as if
dislodged from happiness and grief. Their branches
hang in the broken air, in a space carved out by
words and unmaliciousness. Yet you can hear, just
beyond the horizon, the winter camped like an army
in the distance, conjuring up snow with
its fan-like snow machines: a grammar floating in
with the summerboats, at once too grandiose and

silly. But *here* the business of things continues.
The scattered clusters of construction workers write
epithalamions on their lunch hour, which they pass
back and forth to one another all afternoon. Desire
gets tangled like a kite in the scaffolding. High
up in the difficult air, a thousand birds throw
songs across the sky, epithalamions! And spread
like smoke over everything: the thickness July

is given to, the empty happiness of losing a
job, of masturbating twice in a row. Marriage after
all is like this, or speaking of it is. And thus
this poem, which wanted so badly to leave a perfect
imprint of itself on itself, a key within it to
its own interpretation, a surface and nothing more.
It wanted to leave you that kind of clarity; a city,
if you will, absolutely lit, absolutely still;

something it could offer, imperfect, utterly complete,
and therefore unlike itself. And that's how exact
desire is, how good it feels to have intentions!
But with all the theories and phonecalls, the
different things to eat, to watch on TV, we
sometimes grow confused, get horny, after all,
at the wrong moments. But what will arrest this
play and promiscuity? What will interrupt the
cycles of weather and make them start all over—
as you have, by interweaving the different ways
you talk? Should there be a way of speaking
that is perfectly friendly, an epithalamic
language? Probably not. Should there be
epithalamions? Yes, of course: what else is there?

# APPARATUS FOR WRITING IN THE DARK

> How far from the places where we live
> are these spectacles of love and animosity!
> — JOHN KRICH

1) Here is one way of thinking about longing: The distance between the body and the shadow of the body.

2) Today I fell in love in the laundromat. Perhaps when the book-sized box of *Cheer* slid into the mouth of the vending machine. Perhaps when I was folding a pair of pants, pushing my hands into the damp pockets, reading the washing instructions for the first time.

3) Here's a way of looking at language: A man on the street says, "Could you spare some change? I'm trying to get to Boston. To my wife." You give him "some change." You feel strange and unhappy. You are walking somewhere invisible right now.

4) Today I had lunch with Victoria. I tried to see through her shirt as she chewed on her green beans. It was like kissing a photograph.

5) Here's a way of thinking about poetry: It's past midnight. You lie in bed reading a book about dreams, a glass of milk beside you. It's cold but you keep the window open; the night is large and empty, and helps you, though you're unhappy. Outside the stars are sparkling, pale and tiny, strung up in the sky like the baskets of a ferris wheel. You are floating in an unaccountable solitude. You read with exquisite care. You fall asleep with the lamp on.

Part Three

# THE
# FORBIDDEN
# POEMS

Do not ask for the
knowledge of angels;
it shall not be yours,
and you will only
open the forbidden book.
— TERTULLIAN

# 1.
# Old

You must not have known,
o god, how we feared this.

— IGNATIUS

OF ANTIOCH

## 1)
## HOMECOMING

It began with the very dark and after that
a few searchlights on the horizons. A hand
pushed something forth. Water? Food?
A will shaped like a hook?
                              Great forests
were confiscated, their roots tangled
in nothingness, their stones sleeping
in broken rows. And overhead a few
more firmaments clicked on: unfathomable.

2)
DAY


And it was said: *Let us make something*
*in our likeness and give it the good clay*
*under the scales of the endless plowland,*
*a home in a dead breeze, a man*
*on a bed of thorns, a ruse inside the world.*

3)
ADAM


He heard the wind
pulling itself tentatively
through the rocks: it was
your hair, lord. He watched a hill
change in the dawnlight:
another plan you abandoned.
What the new edges
of his hands touched
was always you, good
to look at, strange, immortal.

But when he slept
the little intervals
of his breathing, the minutes
of his dreams burned away.

4)
## THE DEMONS

Few are the things the unhappy host of angels
took along with them when in a huff you threw
the reckless lot and all their big plans down
onto the smoking floor of hell;
                                    but infinite
their tools to fashion traps for us! O infinite
and strong their hands, and sweet and full
their perfect voices, together in our tiny ears!

## 5)
## LAMENT

O what the demons must have spent
to rise out of noise and darkness without
bottom through the tall, unholy smoke!
Though afterwards, together with their
abandoned wings, they'd forgotten
all about it. For the boy
went forth and worked dumbly and figured
nothing out. And the girl
wasn't yet within the strange robe
of her body and came and gave
to him the story of the snake
that under the thin leaves kissed her.

And all along the demons
dragged themselves across the raped
arena of the world and gathered
and applauded and forgot it all and flew off
in a weak cloud, disappointed! Only death
with its crossed eyes stayed and made a home here.

## 6)
## EXPULSION

There they stood, beyond the gates, a little
destroyed against the old inlands, hating
the beasts crawling about, flying overhead,
themselves running out of common knowledge.
Rattled and confused (for where did this leave them?),
they waited, back to back, looking out:
the dim memory of a girl who gave
birth to someone else's children, and of a boy
who under the cold dirt of the plowland
sunk his hand for the first good time.

And far off, thin and frequent, lightning rubbed
the backs of the fields beyond the fields:
a kind of accident they began slowly
to notice, though everything at once
called out under the same strange infamy.

7)
STORM

Noah was cold with wind and wind
and rain hung from his bones.
His ship tossed like a leaf on creaking
boards and, far off, a raven dropped
from its beak a branch and flew
away, irritated.
                    The sea leaned
like a wing in the storm and the sharp,
unfiltered air. But o the little,
ridiculous boat pushed forth,
in its famous coat of rain
and wind, in a hurry to get
anywhere at all: a kind of tree
about to snap, a medieval town
on a cliff. And all
the while a family man, a drunk
of sorts, searched for the familiar
holes that gulls, hungry and un-
thinking, carve in the coastal air.

# 8)
## SODOM INVENTORY

From the *Fos Cellarium Fisci*


10,000  pounds of oil
   50  pounds of garum
   35  pounds of pepper
  150  pounds of cumin
    2  pounds of cloves
   30  pounds of costum
    1  pound of cinnamon
   50  pounds of dates
  100  pounds of figs
   30  pounds of pistachios
   10  hogsheads of almonds
  100  pounds of olives
  150  pounds of chick-peas
   20  pounds of rice
   50  pounds of hidrio
   20  skins of Cordova leather
   10  pounds of auro pimentos
   50  quires of papyrus

## 9)
## THE PLAGUE OF FROGS

It was said: *the rivers shall bring*
*forth frogs that will enter your roads,*
*fields, houses, beds, and in your dreams*
*form a blanket that, like the snow*
*deep in winter, will cover the long earth.*

And the sound will be as the sound of hell:
beautiful, endless, with a thousand edges.

## 10)
## AARON

morning by morn-
ing for seven
days under the
open sky, Aaron
cast little stones
at the golden
calf and evening
by evening said
to it: *forgive me.*

## 11)
## JONAH

He crawled from the waves
like an old horse,
and spread out on
the beach, and took

a handful of dark sand
into his mouth, and fell
asleep, the sound of the
blood still spinning
in his blackened arms.

## 12)
## THE ASSYRIANS

tore the clothes from
their backs, spread ashes
on their loins, and
dragged themselves through
the streets of Nineveh,
calling out: *a god has
come whom we have failed.*

# 2.
# New

Saddest of all things, lord,
is the dirt your blood ran down.
—CYPRIAN OF CARTHAGE

# 1)
## THE CHILD

The unlikely view of it!
The flashing sea; what in the bible
look like ordinary birds; a brothel;
a tractor; another artery; a clear
strip of farmland; and off in the distance
a house whose beams are hanging
with their old, ordinary dust.

And all the while, on the floorboards
of a barn, sleeps our lord,
with his little knees up, with his face
and torso up, with his arms
outstretched, uncomfortable: a child!

And outside, beyond him, the oats
in the fields cough up their tight,
unfriendly husks, madly, in separate
puffs: each the kernel of a new
harvest, an uncollected coin
no one thinks very much about.

## 2)
## SIN


Like the blue, unreasonable sheets of ice
that spread out, strong and beautiful,
along the spines of the groaning rivers,
for years our sins covered us
and the parents of us: so cold
if you breathed on them they grew
still colder. For years our limbs clacked
with the weight of them. Our shoulder
blades and the noisy, matted locks
of our hair shook with the sound
of them. For years they hung from our
bones or piled up like heaps of blood
and shit before us, however we turned
or stepped away, or did our chores,
mechanically, out under a tall
and wind-torn sky that flexed its clouds and
made its fists and didn't like us very much.

But one day you arrived, o lord, with your
thin, lit face, like a strange dog over a hill,
and took your chisels to the long floes
of ice that covered us, one by one,
snapping the backs our sins lay out along,
impregnable, disfigured, in their thousands.

## 3)
## CRUCIFIXION

Where did the good men find you, lord? Hiding
behind a rock? Casting out the money-
changers who only wanted to help? Sleeping
in the open belly of the lepers'
den? Were you leaving your promises
and parables behind you, refusing, as usual,
to be specific? Or building another cabinet
out of oak you were not famous for?

O, in the end, only hanging from a cross
under a small, unholy sky that could not
gleam, reflect a single thing, or even
hold its clouds still for the amateur photographers
who swarmed like angels around you, tired
of the worn-out gods, agitated, focusing in.

4)
EVENING


At dusk the sun settles down on a roof
as usual, spitting and foaming like an old mule,
a beast, a sullied thing for which suicide,
sadly, is unthinkable. And though the same
recurs every evening, with the same phrasing,
still, each time, there is something funny
and beautiful about it, something strange
which few have spoken well of. And though all
remember one or two of the more spectacular
sunsets, even if angels failed to show up, or if
the sun descended, slowly and wonderfully,
on what was otherwise the most forgettable day
of the year, still, few, outside of amateur
philosophy and a handful of sonnets,
have thought very much about it: a kind
of ceremony we don't witness very well.

But on the day when the body of you died,
the sun did something terrible which we
will not willingly forget: stopped
in the center of its flight, like a pin
or a nail, took off its clothes and got
into a thousand obscene positions: one of them
crying, one praying and babbling like
an idiot, and one laying its big,
unhappy head on a kind of anvil beneath
the blade of a sharpened, invisible ax.

5)
RELIC


You laid your shroud, o maker, along the white
floodlit earth: a sheet
of sadness in the snow or the snow
itself! Though later, unhappy, you forgot
the entire performance: a good one, overall,
if often it lost its way, got off
its clothes at bad moments, and kicked out
the moneychangers who after all
were very like you. A crowd of Romans,
who'd never seen a field grow or one wall
of Jerusalem hang with rain, hovered about,
guessing, in unnoticeable weather.

When you died, even the rivers responded
by moving along, unchanged. What few
good men were there, in sheets called clothes,
sang from the rooftops how for three days
the broken rows of earth gave you
a grave here. And a handful of kings
stared into the lower brink of hell
that shook with coins their thousand
cartloads could not carry away.

## 6)
## DEATH


O that your death is a short day:
when the moon lies deflated on the winter
ground and with long, used ropes

you are lowered down into a grave;
when the clouds, tired of looking big
and somber, disperse unevenly, heading

nowhere in particular, and the great,
nauseated sea does something it never did
before (gets dreamy and contemplative,

unhappy it wasn't the backdrop of better
poems or paintings or memories than that);
when the walls of your body peel away

in an unfamiliar room and rivers
of air take ahead the emptiness
of your genitals; when the sun

moves under the dirt, slowly and forever,
and death comes striding, bringing
to the sober man its vulgar nothings.

7)
## RESURRECTION

After two days that hung between the dirt
and the sky and, like the stone they dropped
over the mouth of your grave, stood still
and wouldn't budge, you poked a hand up,
an elbow, a strong shoulder, a big, unfathomable
torso, and got yourself altogether up
on two good feet and in a huff dusted off
and walked over the cold, impossibly black earth
we now cannot fully imagine you on:
                                        a day
unlike any other, though on earth the rivers
continued to inch along their terrible,
dried trails, though the clouds moved off
as always and the sun, bright and invisible,
rolled across the middle of the afternoon
above the reckless children in the streets
who had to be told, over and again,
by their silly parents the miracle of it.

## 8)
## ASCENSION


In a cloud you rose, o out of nowhere,
through the tall columns of air the stars
of which cannot be counted they are so beautiful
and intimidating! And at your side
the guardians announced your terrible return
to earth when one day, from the uttermost part
of the air, you will bring not a handful
of promises, as before, nor a body hanging
with real flesh, nor the long, inexplicable
parables we feared and discussed forever,
but only a balance and a shining blade.

## 9)
## THE DISCIPLES

When the disciples, fearless and silly, got
your light in their eyes, they took up
and dashed down the statues of the gods
over the sewer grates of the Roman roads,
proclaiming, insanely, to the people:

*In sin*
*you take the last appendage of the ruined*
*world to bed with you, o wolves! What little*
*you tug out of the dirt you throw to comfort*
*and ease; but you will feel the hunger for what*
*today you waste in tired hallucinations*
*and the pleasure of your limbs which, though*
*beautiful and trimmed, lie heavy in irons.*

*So fuck yourselves who float about, unthinking.*
*The demons wear your clothes and borrow*
*your wives while you lounge around*
*and drink good wine until health be yours!*

# 10)
## SALVATION

O save the plowman and his plow, who tugs
the dirt around all day and, under a sky
that straightens up and twitches like a lunatic,
gives to the crows his day's work. Save
the jackals on the hill with their small
glass statues of gods that used to stand
over the fountains and stone floors of cities
and now lose their edges in the teeth
of the difficult wind. And from the fire
that will race along the runways of the earth,
save the wine that for centuries helped
the men of God to their beautiful contemplations,
save the folding rain and the flowers
of the summer loafing in their millions, save
the 1980 New Orleans Saints, and o, most
of all, save the sea with its old, dead boats,
with its spine and telephone cables broken,
though the sea dislikes us, and every evening
obscenely lowers its tide to the perfect stars.

## 11)
## THE EARTH

O where is that imperfect body you abandoned
the walls of? A grave? Or a hovel? Can you
remember the way you slowly leaned
from a cross and stiffened? How angels wrung
their hands and swirled overhead
and everything fizzled out: a kind
of sadness that now looks good on you?
Do you remember the few cabinets
you fashioned and left here? Or wobbling
down a road with hacks and coughs, birds
and dirt and two old sticks that were
your lungs? Or the tossed house of your body?

For what good, when you return, big and armed,
if you forget the little parables you left here,
or the death that was not yours at all, yourself
a bed, and handful of chances, in a tiny room?

12)
PRAYER


Don't harm the smallest thing on earth, o lord,
a shifting cloud, a house or single boat
or animal or boy or prayer. Don't harm
the thinnest tree; and if midnight hangs
a moon among its boughs, if the harsh,
deliberate wind sweeps out along its leaves
like ice or thoughtless children come and climb
its bending arms, remember how, like us,
it started out, dumb, immortal, good
to look at in your eyes: another gift
you brought to us after you gave us birth.

Don't harm the smallest thing on earth, o lord,
a single farm, a Wilfred Owen line.
But bring again the serious, gentle man
you were, though tenderness was not, admit,
another gift you thought you'd need to bring
to us to whom you'd given air and lungs.
O take the death away that we, somehow,
perpetuate each hour, unto the ground
that each of us will suffer from until
you lift us through the air and space which is
yourself, o lord, and take us home again.

Casey Finch is at work on his
Ph.D. at New York University.

# The Contemporary Poetry Series

EDITED BY PAUL ZIMMER

# The Contemporary Poetry Series

EDITED BY BIN RAMKE

J. T. Barbarese, *New Science*
J. T. Barbarese, *Under the Blue Moon*
Scott Cairns, *The Translation of Babel*
Richard Cole, *The Glass Children*
Wayne Dodd, *Echoes of the Unspoken*
Wayne Dodd, *Sometimes Music Rises*
Joseph Duemer, *Customs*
Casey Finch, *Harming Others*
Norman Finkelstein, *Restless Messengers*
Karen Fish, *The Cedar Canoe*
Caroline Knox, *To Newfoundland*
Patrick Lawler, *A Drowning Man Is Never Tall Enough*
Sydney Lea, *No Sign*
Jeanne Lebow, *The Outlaw James Copeland
   and the Champion-Belted Empress*
Phillis Levin, *Temples and Fields*
Gary Margolis, *Falling Awake*
Jacqueline Osherow, *Looking for Angels in New York*
Donald Revell, *The Gaza of Winter*
Martha Clare Ronk, *Desire in L.A.*
Aleda Shirley, *Chinese Architecture*
Susan Stewart, *The Hive*
Terese Svoboda, *All Aberration*
Arthur Vogelsang, *Twentieth Century Women*
Sidney Wade, *Empty Sleeves*
C. D. Wright, *String Light*